I Can't Sleep

A Division of The McGraw·Hill Companies

Columbus, Ohio

www.sra4kids.com

SRA/McGraw-Hill

A Division of The **McGraw·Hill** Companies

Copyright © 2002 by SRA/McGraw-Hill.

All rights reserved. Except as permitted under the United States Copyright Act, no part of this publication may be reproduced or distributed in any form or by any means, or stored in a database or retrieval system, without prior written permission from the publisher.

Printed in the United States of America.

Send all inquiries to:
SRA/McGraw-Hill
8787 Orion Place
Columbus, OH 43240-4027

ISBN 0-07-569747-5

2 3 4 5 6 7 8 9 DBH 05 04 03 02

Jeepers the steer is going to sleep.
He needs his sleep to feel good in the morning.

But Jeepers keeps peeking!
He just can't seem to fall asleep.

He is too cold.
He pulls his green sheet up to his cheek.
He is too hot.
He kicks the sheet off with his feet.

Jeepers creeps from his stall to seek help from his dad.
"Dad, I can't sleep."

"Go back to your stall and think of sheep.
Think of sheep and you will fall asleep.
You will see."

Jeepers did think of sheep.
Lots and lots of sheep.
But still no rest for Jeepers.